LEADERS OF
ANCIENT EGYPT

SNEFRU | The Pyramid
Builder

LEADERS OF
ANCIENT EGYPT

SNEFRU

The Pyramid Builder

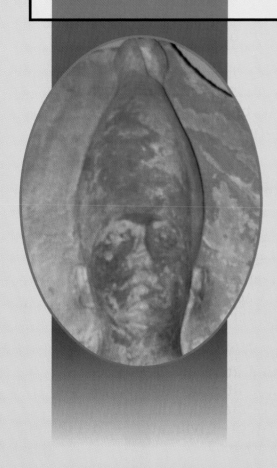

Susanna Thomas

the rosen publishing group's
rosen
central

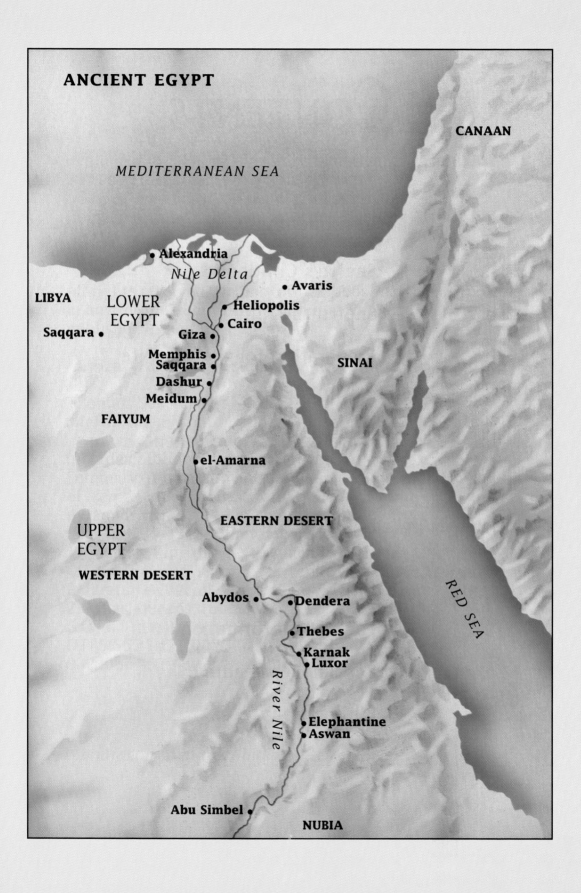

ANCIENT EGYPT

CANAAN

MEDITERRANEAN SEA

• Alexandria

Nile Delta

LIBYA

LOWER
EGYPT

• Avaris

• Heliopolis
• Cairo

Saqqara •

• Giza

Memphis •
Saqqara •
Dashur •
Meidum •

SINAI

FAIYUM

• el-Amarna

EASTERN DESERT

UPPER
EGYPT

WESTERN DESERT

RED SEA

Abydos •

• Dendera

• Thebes
• Karnak
• Luxor

River Nile

• Elephantine
• Aswan

Abu Simbel •

NUBIA

INTRODUCTION

Ancient Egyptian civilization grew and flourished thanks to the unique geographical conditions of the country. Egypt is divided into two parts. The southern half, known as Upper Egypt, consists of a long, narrow strip of fertile land on either side of the river Nile, which flows from south to north. The rest of the land in Upper Egypt consists of desert. There are rocky mountains in the east between the Nile and the Red Sea, but in the west, apart from a few oases, there is nothing but a broad expanse of desert sand. The northern half of the country, known as Lower Egypt, is flat land where the river divides into smaller branches that spread out into a wide V shape. This area is called the Nile Delta.

The idea of two halves making a whole was a common one in ancient Egyptian thought. The

This stone vessel is believed to have been a possession of Snefru's royal family.

country is geographically divided into north and south, and the land itself was seen as divided into the black fertile soil for farming, which was called *kemet*, and the desert, which was called *deshret*. Egyptian kings, who were known as pharaohs, were always called the kings of two lands, and the royal headdress was actually made up of two different crowns, the White Crown of Upper Egypt and the Red Crown of Lower Egypt. The term "pharaoh" comes from the ancient Egyptian word *per-aa*, or "great house," which was actually the name for the Egyptian king's palace.

GOVERNMENT

The pharaoh was the most powerful member of society and was in charge of all religious and political institutions. He selected all the members of the government and all the important priests, who were often members of his own family. The post of king was also considered divine, with the king representing a god called Horus, who was the son of the two important gods Osiris and Isis. One of the pharaoh's titles was Son of Re, showing that the king was also closely associated with the sun god Re. In a spiritual sense, the main role of the king was to maintain *Maat*, which is hard to translate exactly, but includes the ideas of order as opposed to chaos, and a general sense of rightness.

Great emphasis was always placed on the importance of the union of the two lands, indicating that it was essential for the efficient running of the state. The dual nature of the land was almost always respected, with the employment of two viziers (secretaries of state), two treasurers, and sometimes even two complete civil services. The success of this strategy is shown by the fact that the country remained united for most of Egyptian history.

THREE SEASONS

The Egyptian year was divided into three seasons, called inundation (June to September), cultivation (September to April), and harvest

This wall painting from a tomb depicts farmers harvesting grain.

(April to June). The inundation, or flooding, occurred when the Nile increased in volume because of heavy rain from further south in Africa. As the level of the Nile rose, it burst its banks all along the Nile Valley and flooded the surrounding countryside. This water also brought with it large amounts of silt and organic matter, so the land was both watered and fertilized for the coming year. Crops were planted once the waters had receded in the cultivation season. These included cereals such as barley, emmer wheat, and winter wheat, which were used to make bread and beer. Vegetables included lettuce, cucumbers, onions, leeks, beans, and melons. Castor-oil plants produced oil for cooking, medicine, cosmetics, perfume, and fuel to burn in lamps. Herbs and spices were also grown, including dill and saffron. Bees were farmed for honey. Trees grown for their fruit included date-palms, figs, and pomegranates. Grapes were grown on vines for making wine. The

This clay statue portrays a peasant making beer.

Egyptians also enjoyed gardening, and many trees, shrubs, and flowers were grown to fill people's gardens. Flax was a common plant and was used to make linen, which was the main material for clothing, along with wool and leather from sheep and goats. These crops were widely cultivated, as were cattle. With the addition of different sorts of fish that were caught from the Nile and birds found in the region, especially duck, it is clear that the Egyptians enjoyed a rich and varied diet.

BARTER

The Egyptians did not use money. Instead, they used an efficient system of exchanging goods and giving presents known as barter. It is hard for us to imagine how this worked, when today we are used to having both real money in the form of coins and notes, and virtual money in the form of checks and credit cards. Like us, the Egyptians had different values for different objects, so they knew, for example, that a duck was more expensive than a loaf of bread, or that a lump of copper was more valuable than a lump of wood of the same size. The ancient Egyptians had to buy and sell things by keeping in mind the value of everything. If someone did a day's work on a farm, he might be paid with three loaves of bread, six onions, and a pair of sandals, which would all add up to one day's wages. The next day he might be paid in other goods, perhaps ten loaves of bread and a jug of beer, or one goose, which was an expensive item. If the next day he wanted to go shopping to buy a dress for his daughter, then he might pay the shopkeeper with the five leftover loaves of bread that his family hadn't eaten, or perhaps with a couple of heads of lettuce that his wife had grown in their garden.

The things that people offered each other weren't always actual objects. Sometimes people were able to buy and sell things by offering to perform labor or provide services. For example, scribes, who could read and write, were very important and highly thought of because most people could not read or write. Consequently, a scribe wouldn't have to grow his own food or make his own clothes because people would pay him with these things in return for services he performed, such as writing a letter to a cousin who lived in a different town. This cousin in turn would then have to pay a scribe in his town to read the letter to him. This same barter system worked throughout Egyptian society, so everyone from the farmer and his workers to the pharaoh and his architects and statesmen were all paid in this way.

EGYPTIAN HISTORY

Scholars have divided Egyptian history into different periods in order to make it easier to study. The first person to do this was an Egyptian priest called Manetho, who wrote a history of Egypt in Greek for the pharaoh Ptolemy I around 300 BC. Manetho divided the kingdoms of Egypt into about thirty different groups, called dynasties.

A wooden statue of an Old Kingdom official

The divisions were usually based on different ruling families. Egyptian history has also been divided into major periods. The main ones are the Old Kingdom (approximately 2600 to 2150 BC), the Middle Kingdom (approximately 2000 to 1600 BC), and the New Kingdom (approximately 1550 to 1090 BC).

Although Egyptians themselves didn't actually write history books until much later—in the Hellenistic period when they were ruled by Greeks—there are many other ways that we can find out what happened. The evidence comes from paintings, written sources, and archaeological discoveries. We know most about the richest section of society, the elite, because these were the people who could afford to decorate their houses and tombs. These were the only people, apart from scribes, who could read and write. Some information is known about the remaining 99 percent of the population, and this mainly

comes from excava-
tions of their crowded
villages, which are full
of small houses and
cemeteries.

THE EVIDENCE

Pharaohs sometimes
decorated temples
with the names of pre-
vious kings, which are
known as king lists.
Several lists exist. One
of the most extensive
can be seen in the
temple of the Nine-

A painted limestone statue of a
scribe, sitting cross-legged, holding a papyrus scroll.

teenth Dynasty pharaoh Seti I (1294–1279 BC)
at Abydos, which lists seventy-nine kings going
back to the First Dynasty. A list written at
Karnak during the Eighteenth Dynasty lists
sixty-two kings between the First and
Eighteenth Dynasties. Another list was found in
the tomb of a Nineteenth Dynasty scribe called
Tjenroy at Saqqara, and this names fifty-seven
rulers between the First and Nineteenth
Dynasties. A papyrus written in hieratic—
a form of script simpler than hieroglyphics—

now called the Turin Canon, was found in the nineteenth century. This originally listed over three hundred rulers. Unfortunately it was very carelessly handled and is now in a fragmentary condition.

Temples, especially in the New Kingdom, were decorated with paintings and written descriptions of pharaohs defeating the enemies of Egypt. Although these were designed to emphasize the powerful role of the king, and to show that he was maintaining *Maat*, they can also be used to establish what happened in each reign. Tombs of nobles from the Old Kingdom onward were decorated with lots of different scenes and descriptions of daily life. Sometimes they included an autobiography of the tomb occupant, as well as illustrations of the preparations for the tomb occupant's mummification and burial. These scenes often included drawings and names of family members as well as their occupations.

Excavations of temples have shown how Egyptian religion worked and what priests did, while excavations of palaces and towns have given us lots of information about what people's houses and gardens were like, what furniture they had, and what they ate. Excavations of cemeteries have shown us what people thought was important enough to take with them into the afterlife, as well as given us lots of information about burial practices.

SNEFRU

King Snefru reigned during the Old Kingdom of ancient Egypt. Later Egyptians would look back on this era as the "golden age" of Egyptian civilization, when the arts, including language, architecture, sculpture, and painting, were developed to a very high degree. It was also a period when strong rulers led the country and maintained peace and prosperity for the inhabitants. These powerful pharaohs also built many pyramids on the desert edge at the point between the Nile Valley and the delta. It was a period when trading links were forged with other countries in Africa and the Middle East and many luxurious and exotic goods were imported into Egypt.

Snefru was the first pharaoh of the Fourth Dynasty. He ruled for twenty-four years between 2584 and 2560 BC. He built three different pyramids during his lifetime and was the father of Khufu, who built the famous Great Pyramid at Giza. He brought timber from Lebanon and turquoise from the Sinai desert.

The Great Sphinx *(right)* and the Great Pyramid of Khufu at Giza, Egypt

He fought successful campaigns against the Nubians in central Africa and against Libyan tribesmen in the western desert. He is remembered in Egyptian literature as a kind and benevolent ruler.

SNEFRU'S CHILDHOOD

Snefru's father was King Huni, who was the last pharaoh of the Third Dynasty, and his mother was Meresankh I, who was a royal princess and may have been Huni's sister. Throughout Egyptian history, it was normal practice for the pharaoh to marry his own sisters and his own daughters.

Snefru was born and grew up in the royal palace in the capital city of Memphis, near modern-day Cairo. We have no evidence of this palace, but comparison with other sources indicates that it would have been a large, luxurious building. The walls would have been made of mud brick, and the windows would have been set just below the ceiling in order to let in light and cool breezes. It seldom rained in Memphis, and there would also have been living spaces on the roof, which were probably

A sculpture of the pharaoh Snefru, who ruled from 2584 to 2560 BC.

shaded with canopies made of linen and matting. The palace

A stone carving showing cooks preparing and baking bread

compound would have included the main buildings, which would have contained many different suites of rooms, including bedrooms, bathrooms, banqueting halls, and rooms for receiving guests. Some of the rooms would have been open to the sky, perhaps with roofed walkways or colonnades around the edges. The walls and floors of the palace would have been brightly painted with pictures of plants and flowers and geometric patterns. There would have been shallow pools containing water lilies and fish, and gardens full of trees and flowers.

The palace compound would also have housed vegetable gardens, kitchens, and

storerooms full of food, as well as a bakery to make bread and cakes and a brewery to make beer, which was the most common drink. There was probably also a butchery area, where animals either from the palace compound or from surrounding country estates would have been slaughtered and cut up in preparation for cooking. There may also have been a potter's workshop to make all the vessels needed for preparing, cooking, and eating food, as well as to provide lamps, big jars to hold water, and other household items. There may well have been a metalworking area for making and mending copper tools used in the house. There would also have been a laundry, and an area for spinning and weaving wool and linen to make clothing.

All the work of looking after children, preparing food, cooking, and cleaning would have been done by servants. However, royal women were sometimes involved in making and sewing cloth, as needlework was considered a ladylike task.

SCHOOL DAYS

Evidence from later periods suggests that the palace would have been the home for all of the royal women and children, while the pharaoh would have had a number of homes that he used as he traveled around the country. Snefru grew up in an extended family with his mother Meresankh, as well as the other wives of the pharaoh, his brothers and sisters, and probably also various aunts and cousins. He would have gone to school, which was called the "house of instruction," with other boys in the palace compound. There he was taught drawing, painting, mathematics, reading, and writing. There is no evidence that there were specially trained professional schoolteachers during this period, and it is thought that royal uncles and other male relatives probably took charge of instruction at these palace schools. School would have taken place in the morning, as is still the case in Egypt today. Many of the lessons would have taken place outdoors in the fine weather. Boys sat cross-legged in rows on the ground.

Although the Egyptians had invented a very fine sort of paper called papyrus, which was made out of reeds, it was quite expensive to produce. Consequently, students practiced writing on wooden tablets covered in white paint, as well as on scraps of flat stone and pieces of broken pottery. Snefru was taught

both hieratic and hieroglyphic writing. Boys learned to write by copying phrases and exercises. Hieratic was the equivalent of modern handwriting, and it was always written from left to right. Hieroglyphic script consisted of a series of picture symbols and was mainly used to decorate buildings and monuments. Nearly a thousand signs were used during the Old Kingdom. Hieroglyphs were written right to left, left to right, or top to bottom. The signs were written without punctuation or gaps between words, and there were also no vowels. Some signs represented consonants, some represented sounds, and some represented ideas. The Egyptians also loved puns and word games, and many signs have more than one meaning. Most ancient Egyptians couldn't read hieroglyphic writing, but Snefru would have learned at least the basics of the language.

He also learned how to hunt wild animals in the desert, and how to spear fish from a small boat on the Nile. Travel at this time was almost always by water rather than by road, and a canal would have been built joining the Nile to the palace. He would probably have sailed model boats made of wood or papyrus on the canal, and played games like tug-of-war and arm wrestling with his friends. Leather balls have been found that show that boys played various games of catch, and there are also examples of sets of bowling pins from this period. Snefru would have had various wooden toys to play with, as well as a pet hunting dog.

Snefru probably wore a short, knee-length kilt in the summer, which was tied together around his waist. He may have worn a triangular loincloth as underwear, which again would have been tied together. In the winter he probably wore a linen shirt as well, and probably a wool or leather cloak. His sandals would have been made of woven reeds. His hair would have been quite long, and it would have been worn in a plaited bunch on the side of his head.

Probably when he was about twelve years old, this "side-lock" was cut off and he was circumcised, both acts indicating that he was no longer considered a child.

It is not known how often Snefru saw his father, King Huni, or how much preparation he was given for becoming a pharaoh. He would have spent a few teenage years either attached to a temple priesthood, where he would further his academic and religious studies, or in the army, where he would learn fighting skills and how to command men.

MILITARY TRAINING

During the Old Kingdom, there was no need for a permanent standing army in Egypt. Individual local governors and officials had their own small armies or groups of soldiers who kept order. These soldiers also acted as a sort of police force. They guarded important officials and their families, and there is also evidence that they patrolled the desert around each settlement in order to protect against raids from desert bedouins. The king and his palace also had a small troop of bodyguards, as well as a special group of officials who guarded the royal women in the palace harem.

Wooden models of a group of Nubian archers. The ancient Egyptians often hired Nubian soldiers to beef up their army.

There was also a group of officials who arrested and punished people for crimes like nonpayment of taxes. Local rulers also employed mercenaries from Nubia. These men, known as the *medjay*, were famed for their height and strength and were often used as scouts, archers, and light infantry.

Snefru trained with the palace guard and learned how to use a variety of weapons. These included the mace, the ax, the bow and arrow, the spear, and the throw stick. The mace was a simple weapon consisting of a pear-shaped stone head attached to a tapering wooden shaft. It was nevertheless an effective weapon, and there are many pictures of Egyptians hitting their enemies over the head with this club.

Snefru's ax had a semicircular copper head tied to a wooden handle through holes in the metal. This was also used in hand-to-hand fighting. His spears had sharp tips made of copper or flint (a kind of hard, sharp stone) attached to a wooden staff, and were designed to be thrown at the enemy. His bow was made of one piece of wood narrowing at each end and strung with a piece of animal gut. His arrows were made from reeds with flint or hardwood points and three feathers attached at the other end. His throw stick was curved (like a boomerang) and was mainly used for catching birds.

During the Old Kingdom, soldiers didn't wear armor. Snefru's only protection was a large rectangular shield made of cowhide stretched over a wooden frame. This shield had handles carved in the frame and a leather strap so that it could be hung over his shoulders. However, he was pretty safe practicing with the palace troops because they would all have been very careful not to injure a member of the royal family.

SNEFRU THE KING

After ruling for twenty-four years, King Huni died in 2584 BC. We actually know very little about Huni. The Turin Canon and the Saqqara king list both identify him as the last king of the Third Dynasty and the father of Snefru. His name is also inscribed on a piece of red granite found at Elephantine (near Aswan), suggesting that he built a fortress there on the southern border of Egypt. His tomb has never been positively identified, but it is likely that he was buried either at Meidum in the Faiyum region or at Saqqara near the step pyramid of Djoser.

ROYAL NAMES

Snefru became king after the death of his father, Huni, and it is thought that he ascended to the throne of Egypt in either his late teens or early twenties. One important aspect connected with his coronation was choosing what his royal names would be.

Snefru, like all other Egyptians, received his first name when he was born. However, when he became king he needed new names to express his identity as king. These new names distinguished him from ordinary human beings, and in one sense they acted exactly like his crowns and his robes of state by symbolizing his

The falcon headdress from the statue of Horus found at the temple dedicated to him at Hierakonpolis

high status and royal authority. These names were accompanied by special royal titles, which were Horus, He of the Two Ladies, Horus of Gold, King of Upper and Lower Egypt, and Son of Re.

The title Horus identified the king as an incarnation of the falcon god Horus, who was god of the sky and also the embodiment of divine kingship. Egyptian kings were known as the living Horus. The second title, He of Two Ladies, represented the cobra goddess Wadjet of Buto in the delta and the vulture goddess Nekbet of El-Kab near Luxor. These two towns were major royal centers from the late pre-dynastic period onward, and this title emphasized the dual nature of Egypt. The third title, Horus of Gold, also showed the godlike nature of the king by associating his name with gold, which is yellow like the sun and eternal like the flesh of the gods. The fourth title again shows the dual nature of Egypt as represented by two symbols, the sedge (Upper Egypt) and the bee (Lower Egypt). The fifth title, Son of Re, shows a direct divine origin for the king as the child of the sun god.

In later periods, the particular identity and interests of the king were often reflected in the names the new ruler selected. Snefru chose "Lord of Maat" for both his Horus name and his He of Two Ladies name. We do not know if he had a Horus of Gold name or a King of Upper and Lower Egypt name, and it is possible that he used these titles on their own. His Son of Re name, and the one by which he was most often known, remained Snefru.

ROYAL MARRIAGES

Snefru's main wife, who he married before ascending the throne, was a princess called Hetepheres, who was also the daughter of his father, Huni, although they had different mothers. Snefru also had other wives; some were daughters of Egyptian nobles and possibly

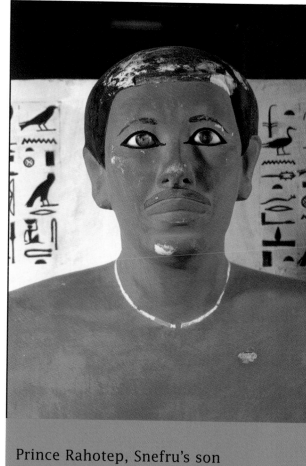

Prince Rahotep, Snefru's son

some of his other sisters. It is known that he had at least three sons, Khufu, Nefermaat, and Rahotep, and also many daughters, including one called Merytyetes.

The ancient Egyptians did not have weddings in the way that we know them today. There is no evidence that they had any sort of marriage ceremony, and from the richest people

A painted relief sculpture of men at work in an Egyptian shipyard

to the poorest, marriage was simply achieved by two people setting up house together. Marriages were often arranged by parents, who would have wanted to gain the best possible partners for their children. First cousins often married each other (as still happens in modern Egypt) in order to keep property within a family.

Because women sometimes owned their own property, rich couples often signed written contracts deciding how the property would be divided and what would happen if they separated. Divorce was quite common, in which case a woman was either given back any property brought to a marriage, or was compensated in some way. There

Egyptian farmers driving cattle across a ford.

was also sometimes a distinction between couples who lived together and those who were married. Men usually had only one wife at a time, although some rich men sometimes also had harems, with other wives or mistresses.

Evidence from poetry, stories, and illustrations of everyday life shows that the Egyptians thought that to be married and have children was the normal way of life and the one that made people happy. Ordinary Egyptians did not usually marry their blood relatives, such as

brothers marrying sisters or fathers marrying daughters. However, there is a lot of evidence to show that pharaohs often married royal princesses who were their sisters and sometimes their daughters. Although this custom may seem very strange to us today, there are various reasons why it did not seem strange to the Egyptians themselves.

One reason was that the pharaoh's main wife, who was called the "great royal consort," often played a very important role in various state festivals and religious ceremonies. A royal princess would probably have been trained from an early age on how to do these jobs. It is clear, however, that such marriages were more than just symbolic, as one of the main roles of the royal wife was to give the pharaoh an heir, and there are many examples of the pharaoh and his sister/wife or his daughter/wife having children.

There were various advantages for the pharaoh in marrying women of the royal family.

Farmers making haystacks

Children born from these marriages would be doubly royal and so would have the strongest claim to the throne. Snefru and his sister/wife Hetepheres had a daughter called Merytyetes and a son called Khufu who married each other, and Khufu went on to inherit the throne from his father. It also got rid of the problem of Egyptian princesses who married

outside the royal family, and whose husbands, either from the ranks of the Egyptian nobility or from foreign royal families, might try and claim the Egyptian throne.

Another reason that the royal family practiced marriage like this was to show that they were like the gods of Egypt. Incest commonly occurred in the myths of Egyptian gods. The main "holy family" consisted of the gods Osiris, Isis, and their son, Horus. Osiris and Isis were brother and sister and married each other, and the pharaoh was the symbolic version of their son, Horus, on Earth.

In the same way, a "great royal wife" who was the daughter of a pharaoh would have been the daughter of a god. If she married her brother, she would be the wife of a god, and if they had children, who became heirs to the throne, she would also be the mother of gods. Consequently, the practice of incest may have been another way of setting the king and his family high above the rest of his Egyptians subjects.

As a final note, it is worth remembering that although Egyptian princesses often married their pharoah brothers, pharaohs also had many other wives, some coming from their own family, some from other important Egyptian families, and still others who were the daughters of foreign rulers.

PREPARATION FOR THE AFTERLIFE

Early in his reign, Snefru decided that he would follow the tradition started by his Third Dynasty ancestor Djoser and build a pyramid to be buried in. Snefru was the greatest pyramid builder in Egyptian history and, for reasons that are not clear, ended up constructing not one, but three pyramids during his lifetime. Although we have no trace of Snefru's body, it is thought that he was probably buried in the last pyramid that was built, the Red Pyramid at Dahshur.

His first pyramid was built at Meidum, which is near the mouth of the Faiyum River. It is not known why Snefru chose this site, which is much farther south than previous royal burial sites at Saqqara. However, it is possible that Snefru was fond of the area and that this was already the site of one of his palaces.

The pyramid and surrounding temple complex at Meidum, the first pyramid that Snefru built

During the Old Kingdom, pharaohs were buried in an area now called the Memphite Necropolis, which spreads along the edge of the desert west of modern-day Cairo. When talking about pyramids, it is important to remember that they were not just single, isolated structures. Each pyramid was surrounded by a small town. A "pyramid complex" included a number of features. There was the main pyramid, of course, and the mortuary temple attached to the base of the pyramid where priests said prayers and brought offerings of food and drink every day for the *ka*, or soul, of the dead king. There were smaller "satellite"

A closer view of the ruins of the temple complex surrounding the pyramid of Djoser at Saqqara, Egypt

pyramids around the main pyramid where the pharaoh's wives were buried. A valley temple, built by the bank of a canal especially cut from the river Nile, was where the body of the dead king was first brought from the capital of Memphis. It was also the location of a number of statues of the dead king, so people who were not allowed into the mortuary temple could still make offerings to him. A causeway linked the valley temple to the mortuary temple. There were rows of mastaba tombs, rectangular buildings named for the Arabic word for bench, where less important members of the pharaoh's family, courtiers, and government officials were buried. These tombs were usually given away as presents by the king, and there was probably stiff competition for them because most people wanted to be as close as possible to the king. There was also a village where all the priests and officials who looked after the everyday running of the temples lived. And there was a small palace for the king to stay in when he came to see how the construction was coming along.

In order to build each of his pyramids, Snefru commissioned a person to act as "overseer of all the King's works." It was this person's responsibility to organize the quarrying

The false door of the pyramid of Djoser at Saqqara

of blocks. These were limestone blocks quarried locally. The best quality blocks of stone were brought from a large quarry at Tura on the east bank of the Nile near Memphis. These were smoothed and polished to a high shine before being used both as the outer casing of the pyramids and to line the walls of the rooms inside.

We are not completely sure how the stone was actually dug out of the hillsides. The most likely method was one where squares were first drawn on the side or top of the rock, and each block was then dug around using hard stone tools, perhaps made of flint. When most of the sides had been freed from the rock face, the block was levered away with wooden poles. Another theory is that small grooves were cut around all the visible sides of the block with handheld copper chisels banged in by hard stone hammers. Wooden wedges were then driven into these grooves and soaked with water, which made the wood expand and so split the piece of stone away from the face of the rock.

Each stone was then hauled away from the quarry on a wooden sledge. Once the stone arrived at the site of the pyramid, either by being dragged overland or brought by barges along the river, the sides and edges were chiseled smooth and the stone was put into place.

There is a lot of debate today over how the pyramids were actually constructed. Archaeological work at the Bent Pyramid at Dahshur shows that the pyramid was built straight onto the desert sand. The great weight of the stones meant that the sand started shifting and

A bas-relief of sculptors at work creating a bas-relief wall sculpture.

sinking, which no doubt contributed to the cracking of the building. For the Red Pyramid, a foundation platform of several layers of white limestone was first laid down.

The most likely method of construction was one where stones were pulled and pushed up a ramp or series of ramps that were built against the face of the pyramid. There are many different theories as to what type of ramp was used. These include a single straight ramp against one side, a spiral ramp following the four sides, and a ramp that zigzagged up one side, or perhaps a combination of some of these ideas. Such a ramp would have been made out of limestone chips and some sort of plaster to hold the chips together.

The individual blocks would have been pulled up a ramp by a group of men holding ropes tied around the blocks. They may also have been pushed from below. The blocks were probably sitting on wooden tracks (like a railroad), soaked with buckets of water to make them slippery. The stones were then laid in horizontal layers with the outermost stone carved with a sloping face along one edge. The pyramid was completed with a single pyramid-shaped stone, known today as the capstone or pyramidion.

WHY BUILD A PYRAMID?

The first and most obvious reason that the pyramids were built was that they were an enormous and visible sign of the wealth and power of the pharaohs. When Snefru built his pyramids, they were the biggest man-made stone buildings in the world. If you were to visit the pyramids today, the first thing you would notice is their size.

It was also thought that the pharaoh's body would be safe for eternity hidden in a pyramid. An important part of Egyptian belief in the afterlife required that the pharaoh's mummified body remain untouched on Earth. Sadly, this turned out not to be the case, as all the pyramids were robbed soon after completion, probably by the workmen who had helped build them in the first place!

The pyramids also served various religious purposes. The Egyptians had a number of different religious beliefs and myths, not all of which made sense when taken together. This was mainly because they liked to hang on to old ideas even when new ones appeared. One of the creation myths of Egyptian religion was that the world first rose out of waters called Nun as a mound or hill. The sun, in the form of the sun god Re, was born on this mound, and so day began. It is possible that the pyramids may have represented this mound.

The first pyramid, built during the Third Dynasty by King Djoser (2638–2619 BC), was made with a series of steps rather than sloping sides. It is possible that this was meant to be a giant staircase for the pharaoh to climb up to heaven so he could become a star. True

thought important enough to record, and it indicates that this ship was a very important vessel.

Because of the very dry conditions of Egypt's climate and the preserving nature of sand, archaeologists have actually discovered and excavated some examples of wooden boats made at this time. One of the most famous of

The funerary boat, complete with oars, of the pharaoh Khufu, Snefru's son, discovered at Giza in 1954

these boats is a large cedarwood rowing boat found next to the Great Pyramid of Khufu at Giza. In 1954, an Egyptian archaeologist named Kamal el-Mallakh uncovered a large oblong pit covered in stone slabs. When one of these was removed, a large cavity was revealed containing planks of wood, rope, matting, and oars. This proved to be the carefully dismantled remains of a boat. A team of restorers working under Hag Ahmed Youssef Moustafa took many years to put the boat back together, and it was finally placed on show to the public in 1971.

The boat is built from thick cedar planks, which were tied together with linen ropes. It has no mast or sail and was propelled by twelve oars. There were five oars down each side of the boat and two large oars at the stern (back) of the vessel, which were used to steer. On the deck there is a small wooden canopy at the bow (front) of the boat to protect a lookout or pilot from the sun. In the middle of the deck there is a large central cabin divided into two rooms. This is surrounded by a framework of wooden poles that would have supported a sunshade made from either linen or reed mats. The boat also contained a wooden gangplank that would have been extended for getting on and off. The vessel is 143 feet long, and it is probably very similar to the one built by Snefru and described on the Palermo Stone.

Snefru concentrated on expanding the capital city at Memphis. He built a fine new palace for himself and his family. The year after he built his big ship, he had enough cedarwood left to build huge wooden doors for the gates of his palace. The Palermo Stone records the "erection of 'Exalted is the White Crown of Snefru upon the Southern Gate' and 'Exalted is the Red Crown of Snefru upon the Northern Gate.'"

The pyramid at Meidum was converted from a step pyramid to a true pyramid with sloping sides.

THE PYRAMID AT MEIDUM

Snefru now had enough men and materials to continue the construction of his pyramid at Meidum. Some archaeologists used to think that the pyramid at Meidum was originally started by Snefru's father, Huni, for himself. This is mainly because a tomb for Huni has not been found. However, the ancient name of Meidum was "Snefru Endures," and Snefru's name has been found written on scraps of stone that were instructions for workers at the site, so it seems likely that he started building the pyramid from the beginning.

A relief sculpture showing workers weaving and making papyrus

The pyramid at Meidum started off as a step pyramid similar to that built by the pharaoh Djoser at Saqqara. During the first half of Snefru's reign,

the first five of seven steps were built, before a change of plans led to these steps being covered over with eight bigger steps. At this point, the pyramid was finished, and Snefru started to build another at Dahshur. However, in the last years of his reign, workmen used stones to fill in the steps of the Meidum pyramid in order to turn it into what is known as a true pyramid, with smooth sloping slides.

The secret burial chamber was probably built first, with the pyramid then constructed on top. The burial chamber was originally entered through a small passage that began in the middle of the north wall of the pyramid. This passage descended through the body of the pyramid for 190 feet. At the bottom of the slope, there is a level corridor 31 feet long. At the end of this corridor, a vertical shaft goes up about 20 feet into the floor of the burial chamber, which is 19 feet long and 8 feet wide.

There are two small rooms off the corridor that originally stored large stone slabs, which were to be dropped into place to block the passageway to the tomb once the king's body had been put inside. However, it seems that no one was ever actually buried in this pyramid. There is still some evidence of the pyramid complex, with traces of the mortuary temple, a satellite pyramid, and the causeway leading to the valley temple.

FAMILY TRAGEDIES

During the first part of Snefru's reign, when it was thought that he was going to be buried in the Meidum pyramid, at least two of Snefru's sons died. There are a number of mastaba tombs to the north of the pyramid, and these include the burial sites of two sons of Snefru called Nefermaat and Rahotep. Both of these tombs are famous because of the objects found in them.

The tomb of Nefermaat and his wife, Atet, was decorated with colorful scenes of daily life for them and their children. These include pictures of men hunting birds in marshland and

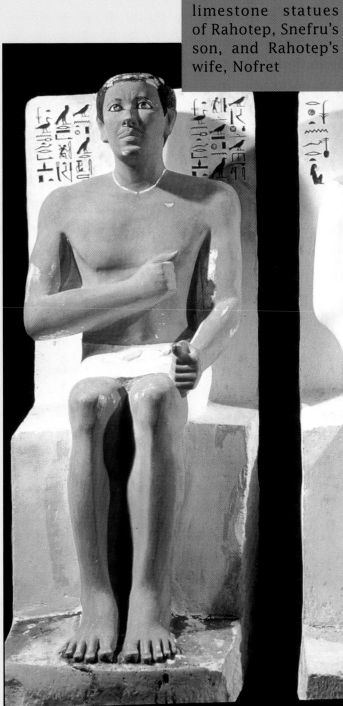

Life-size painted limestone statues of Rahotep, Snefru's son, and Rahotep's wife, Nofret

farmers ploughing and sowing seed. The tomb of Rahotep and his wife, Nofret, contained statues of the couple sitting down. These are made of limestone and are painted in a very lifelike way. Rahotep has reddish brown skin, short black hair, and a little mustache. He is wearing a knee-length kilt and a necklace with a small heart charm on it. Nofret has pale yellowish skin and a black, shoulder-length wig. She is wearing a white dress with shoulder straps and a white cloak. She also wears a large colorful necklace that matches her headband. Both figures are wearing black eye makeup, which was used to help cut down the bright glare of the sun.

RUNNING THE GOVERNMENT

Evidence from private tombs surrounding the king's pyramids indicates that Snefru ran a highly efficient government. Snefru appointed a large number of officials, who were mainly from his own extended family. He supervised their training and gave them presents of land on which to build their houses. Snefru also paid for many of the officials' burial sites in mastaba tombs around his three pyramid complexes.

The central government was run from the king's palace complex at Memphis, where a series of official buildings surrounded the royal residence. The dual nature of the country was represented by certain dual titles and offices. Government departments included the treasury (with the power to tax), the armory, the granaries (also with the power to tax, in the form of expropriations

Methen also describes the rewards given to him by Snefru throughout his career, which included a large house and grounds. "There were conveyed to him as a reward 200 *stat* of land . . . a mortuary offering of 100 loaves every day from the mortuary temple of the mother of the king's children, a house 200 cubits long and 200 cubits wide (235 square feet) . . . Very plentiful trees and vines were set out, a great quantity of wine was made there."

DEALING WITH THE LIBYANS

As well as supervising the construction of his pyramid and running his government, Snefru still had to concentrate on international affairs. The Palermo Stone records that Snefru led campaigns against the Tjehenu, that is, the Libyans, who were a group of tribesmen who lived in the desert west of Egypt. The Libyans were nomadic, which means that they had not settled in one place, but lived in tents with their families and their possessions, including their animals, and moved around from place to place. The Tjehenu were depicted as bearded and light skinned, sometimes with blue eyes. They are recognizable in Egyptian illustrations by blue tattoos, long cloaks, penis sheathes,

pointed beards, long curls hanging on one side of their heads, and often with an ostrich feather in their hair.

Relief sculptures of four figures representing high-born captives, the enemies of Egypt. The tattooed figure is a Libyan, and the bearded figure is a Syrian prince. The other two figures are Nubians.

In later periods of Egyptian history, the Tjehenu and other groups called the Tjemehu, the Meshwesh, and the Libu (the origin of the modern-day name Libya) joined together to attack Egypt. But during the Old Kingdom, the Libyans did not pose any serious threat to the

A limestone stele, or tablet, showing the manufacture of weapons

stability or safety of Egypt. However, Snefru organized a series of raids against these tribes to ensure that they kept away from the Nile Valley. Although the Libyans did not have many material goods to trade with the Egyptians, the feathers often worn in their hair show that they had access to ostriches that also lived in the desert. The Egyptians wanted ostrich feathers to make fans and headdresses and ostrich eggs for food. Ostrich eggs are very large, up to ten inches long, and one ostrich egg can make an omelette for twelve people.

IMPERIAL EXPANSION

The closest country on Egypt's southern border was Nubia. Nubia occupied what is modern-day Sudan, as well as the southern part of modern Egypt now submerged under Lake Nasser. Egypt had been trading with Nubia from late predynastic times, when the

A relief carving showing a victorious pharaoh inspecting the decapitated bodies of his enemies. Note how the king, in typical Egyptian fashion, is made bigger than other figures.

Egyptians wanted the luxury goods native to that country, such as gold, ivory, and ebony. However, during the Old Kingdom, there was an increase in demand in Egypt for raw materials because of the strain of monumental building projects. This meant that Nubia was viewed as a source of goods to be taken rather than bought. Snefru was planning the construction of his enormous pyramid at Meidum,

as well as new palaces and temples in Memphis. These buildings all needed not only gold and precious materials to decorate them, but also large numbers of workers to undertake the work of actual construction.

Consequently, Snefru gathered an army, drawing from all the various local forces and also by recruiting some mercenaries. He appointed a commander who was known as the Overseer of Soldiers. This fighting force was then sent by boat up the Nile to Nubia. The Nubians were not actually any threat to the Egyptian state at this stage, and this action represented a policy of imperialist domination. It was the first of a number of vigorous military campaigns against Nubia where captives, cattle, and wood were taken. A special type of stone called diorite, used for making statues, was now available from Nubian quarries along the Nile. While in Nubia, the Egyptian army built a small settlement at Buhen near the second Nile cataract, about 250 miles south of the existing border at Aswan, where Huni had previously erected a fortress. The Palermo Stone records that the Egyptians returned with 70,000 living prisoners and 200,000 large and small cattle.

These huge numbers illustrate the devastating effect the Egyptian military action must have had on the population of Nubia. Whole villages were wiped out as men, women, and children were taken to Egypt. The men would have worked in the army or on building projects, or they would have been turned into farmers in the Nile Delta. The women and children would have been used as servants in houses or put to work in small businesses like bakeries or breweries. For those Nubians left behind, the loss of their cattle would have taken away one of their main sources of food and wealth.

THE PALERMO STONE

The Palermo Stone was a stele, a standing slab of stone inscribed with writing. This stone is our main source of information for the events of Snefru's reign. Unfortunately, it was smashed into pieces at some time in the past. The Palermo Stone was erected during the Fifth Dynasty, at least 100 years after the death of Snefru. It was inscribed with a set of royal annals, a list of the main events that happened in each year, going back to the beginning of Egyptian history. The object was originally over six feet high, but only a few fragments remain today. Some of these fragments list events that occurred during Snefru's reign.

EXPEDITIONS TO THE SINAI DESERT

Copper was needed in order to make weapons for the army. The source for this metal was far off in the Sinai desert. This area also contained turquoise, which is a blue or green gemstone that the Egyptians loved to use both in jewelry and to decorate small objects and pieces of furniture. One of the ancient Egyptians' favorite combinations of materials was green turquoise from the Sinai mountains, red carnelian from pebbles in the eastern desert, and dark blue lapis lazuli imported from distant Afghanistan. These materials were strung together as beads for necklaces and bracelets or used as colorful inlays in gold headdresses and rings. Sometimes these stones were imitated by colored glass. This was done so cleverly that it is often difficult to tell them apart. Both men and women throughout Egyptian history wore jewelry.

A bas-relief showing workers shaping wood for use in shipbuilding.

The mountains of the Sinai desert had been a source of copper and turquoise since the predynastic period. The ancient Egyptians sent expeditions of miners and quarry workers into the region. Getting to the Sinai involved a long trip, first over land across the eastern desert from the Nile Valley to the coast of the Red Sea, and then by ship to reach the west coast of the Sinai. Here the Egyptians would have unloaded their supplies of food, tools, and weapons, and also the donkeys that they brought with them to carry their tools to the turquoise quarry sites.

There is archaeological evidence from the period of Snefru's reign of campsites and mines

at a site called Wadi
Maghara, which is
140 miles west of

A relief sculpture of a ship
transporting goods

Cairo. Copper-working also took place at this
site, which indicates that the Egyptians probably also mined copper, as well as bought it
from local tribesmen. There are also some fine
pictures carved into rock walls of the pharaoh
beating foreign captives. Snefru is shown wearing a crown and holding a mace above his head,
ready to bring it down on a kneeling bedouin
tribesman whom he is holding by the hair. An
accompanying inscription lists the king's
names and titles.

These pictures and inscriptions indicate
that skilled craftsmen were included in the

teams who went to the Sinai and that they must have occasionally had spare time on their hands for artistic creation. On the return journey, the donkeys would carry the copper and turquoise to the ships, where everything would be loaded on board and sailed back to the east coast of Egypt.

More pyramid building

In the fifteenth year of his reign (2569 BC), for some reason Snefru changed his mind about where he wanted to be buried, and he began to build another pyramid twenty-five miles north of Meidum at Dahshur. However, he was not happy with this new pyramid, and when it was finished he built yet another pyramid, again at Dahshur. This was not the end of the story, because after the third pyramid at Dahshur was finished, he sent workmen back to Meidum to complete the first one! All three pyramids were originally constructed out of local limestone, with highly polished white limestone slabs coating the outer surfaces. This outer layer was very attractive, but it has almost completely disappeared over the centuries as it was stripped away to be used for other building projects.

The Bent Pyramid at Dahshur

THE BENT PYRAMID AT DAHSHUR

When Snefru started building his second pyramid at Dahshur, no one had ever made one with smooth sides like this before. It was started with very steep sides, but problems soon occurred. Cracks developed in the outer face and the internal corridors of the pyramid. To counter this, workmen built an extra layer around the outside of the pyramid, which made it bigger and gave it a gentler slope. However, fresh cracks appeared, and so the top half of the slope was finished with an even shallower incline. This gave the side of the pyramid a curved or bent appearance as the slope changed.

This pyramid is also unique because it has not one but two secret burial chambers with two separate entrances, one on the north face and one on the east face. The north burial chamber and passage were probably constructed before the pyramid was built over it. The passage descends for 240 feet from the entrance. At the bottom, there is a long narrow room with a 40-foot-high corbeled roof, which is formed from slabs of stone protruding from the walls and narrowing the roof space like an arch. The burial chamber is next to and above this room, and was probably originally reached by a ladder. This room also has a corbeled roof 57 feet high.

A second, similarly constructed burial chamber lies above and southeast of the first chamber. A roughly cut corridor now joins the two, but originally the only access to this second chamber was through a passage leading from an entrance on the west side of the pyramid. This passage slopes down for 212 feet before flattening out into a 66-foot-long corridor. This flat corridor contained two large stone slabs, called portcullises, which were meant to be slid across to block off the corridor once the burial was in place. One of these had been closed and disguised with plaster. This was to fool robbers into thinking that they had reached the end of the corridor. It is not known why this pyramid has two burial chambers, and in fact there is no evidence that anyone was ever buried there.

The pyramid complex at Dahshur is better preserved than the one at Meidum. We can see the remains of the mortuary temple at the foot of the eastern side of the Bent Pyramid, as well as the causeway leading to the valley temple. The valley temple itself was vandalized and destroyed at some time in the past, but some of the carvings from the walls are quite well preserved.

THE RED PYRAMID AT DAHSHUR

Perhaps because he was not satisfied with the various changes to the design of the Bent Pyramid, before it was even completed Snefru embarked on the construction of yet another pyramid, again at Dahshur. From the beginning, this one was constructed with a gentler slope, more like the upper section of the Bent Pyramid. Today it is known as the Red Pyramid because of the reddish color of the limestone used in the core. The white limestone surface that originally covered the

pyramid has long
since worn away. The

pyramid was originally 343 feet high, and each side was 722 feet long at the base.

A corridor starting in the north face of the pyramid descends for 206 feet through the core. This flattens out into a corridor 24 feet long that enters the first chamber, which is an oblong room 27 feet by 12 feet, with a corbeled roof 40 feet tall. A short passage then leads to a second room, again with a roof 40 feet tall. A secret passage starts 25 feet above the floor, high up in the wall of this second chamber. It is 24 feet long and leads into the burial chamber. This is a big room measuring 14 feet by 28 feet, and it is 50 feet tall.

After the funeral, the entrance to the secret passage would have been disguised to look like the rest of the blank wall. Unfortunately, however, at some point in the past this passage was discovered by tomb robbers, and when excavators cleared the burial chamber in 1950, all they found were a few fragments of human remains. Nevertheless, it is thought that Snefru was probably buried in this pyramid, and it is possible that these are the remains of his mummy. There is some evidence of the pyramid complex, but the mortuary temple and the valley temple were hurriedly finished, suggesting that Snefru died before they were completed.

Pyramid towns developed around each pyramid as it was constructed. To begin with, towns were needed to house the many thousands of people who were building the whole pyramid complex. This included the men who cut and shaped the blocks, the men who dragged them into place, the architects and designers who checked that everything was working properly, and all the special tradesmen who looked after all the tools that were used, mending those that were broken and constantly making new ones. Some of these people would have been based near the pyramids all year–round, and some would have come only during the inundation season, when they couldn't work on their own farms at home.

All the other people who looked after the workers also lived in these towns. These included bakers to make all the bread and beer that the workers ate and drank. Evidence from the pyramid town of Snefru's son, Khufu, also shows that masses of fish were eaten, and a factory site has been found where thousands of catfish were cleaned, skinned, and had their bones taken out. There were many butchers to kill and process animals that were brought to the site for food. Many of the workmen would probably have brought their wives and children to live with them, and all the activities of a normal town would have taken place, with markets, schools, pottery factories, and temples for worship. Building a pyramid would have been quite dangerous work, with the possibility of falling off the pyramid or the ramps, or being crushed by one of the huge blocks, and there are also examples of large graveyards connected with these pyramid towns. Common people, unlike the royals, were not mummified during this period, and many hundreds of skeletons have been found in the town near Khufu's pyramid. Analysis of these bones has

A bas-relief sculpture of masonry workers going to work

shown that many of the workers had suffered from arthritis and joint disease, especially in their backs—not surprising if you consider the amount of hard manual labor involved.

After the pyramid had been completed, many of the workmen would have packed up and either moved on to the next large building project or gone home to their villages and farms. However, a group of people would have

stayed and lived near the pyramid in order to run religious services that took place every day. Scraps of papyrus found near the pyramid of the Fifth Dynasty pharaoh Neferirkara give some clues of what these priests actually did. There was a permanent group of priests known as servants of the god as well as five groups of priests, each divided into two smaller groups, who took turns serving in the pyramid complex for one month in ten. This meant that for the rest of the year these people could go to their homes and work there.

Their jobs included assisting in the daily rituals in the temple and looking after all the provisions that came to the pyramids. The rituals included washing and dressing statues of the king, and then chanting prayers in front of the statues while burning incense. Food and drink were then offered to the statues. After a short while, the sacred essence of this food was thought to have gone magically into the statues of the king, and so the actual provisions were taken away and eaten by the priests. All this took place up to five times every day.

THE BENT PYRAMID VALLEY TEMPLE FRIEZES

One of the problems that Snefru had to think about was who was going to look after his pyramid complexes after he died. The priests who worked at the pyramid temple were meant to take offerings of food and drink to the *ka*, or soul, of the king every day forever and ever. That meant that the offerings had to be provided, and the priests had to be paid, as did the gardeners, cleaners, and other people who looked after the complex. They were all paid with goods rather than money. This might include bread and beer, meat and vegetables, and new clothes and shoes.

The pharaoh could have hoped that future kings would continue to pay all these people. However, a safer way to ensure continuing prayers at his temple was to set up a system of support that did not rely on the good will of his descendants. Remember that the pharaoh was the biggest landowner in Egypt and owned large numbers of farms and estates all over Egypt. Snefru solved the problem by giving a large number of these estates to his pyramids. This meant that instead of having a human landlord, all the farmers who worked on these lands paid their rent to the pyramid in the form of goods that they had produced.

Rows of illustrations on the walls of Snefru's valley temple show exactly how this happened. Each estate is represented as a woman holding a tray full of offerings, with the name and location of each estate written in front. This system shows us that each of the pyramids created employment for many thousands of people. Resources belonging to the king in the form of food and drink produced on different farms all over the country were brought to one central place. Here they were distributed to all the workers as payment for their services. Consequently, the pyramids represent not only an incredible example of mass organization of people and materials, but also a very successful form of an economy based on the redistribution of goods. We don't know how many people it actually took to build each pyramid, but it has been estimated that between 20,000 and 30,000 men worked in three-month shifts, meaning that nearly 100,000 people were employed each year. They and their wives and families were thus directly bound to the power of the king.

DEATH OF THE KING

After a long and successful reign, King Snefru died in 2560 BC. He was succeeded by his son Khufu, who is still famous today as the builder of the Great Pyramid at Giza, which is one of the seven wonders of the ancient world.

TOMB OF HETEPHERES

Although archaeologists have not been able to find much evidence of the actual burial of Snefru, a lucky accident revealed a wonderful group of objects originally belonging to his wife Hetepheres. In 1925, a team from Harvard University was working at the Great Pyramid at Giza built by King Khufu, the son of Snefru and Hetepheres. One day a photographer's tripod "struck a curious patch of plaster." This turned out to conceal the top of a burial shaft. Investigation revealed a hidden burial chamber containing a sarcophagus (a box to put a coffin in) and various pieces of furniture and funeral equipment. Many of the objects were originally covered in gold foil but were in a very poor state because all the wood parts had long since rotted away. However, after years of painstaking reconstruction, we can now see the furniture that belonged to Hetepheres, including a bed, chairs, boxes, and an elaborate frame to hold up a tent around her bed. Inscriptions on many of the objects show that they had been given to Hetepheres by Snefru and Khufu.

This discovery created a couple of new mysteries. First, why was the wife of Snefru buried with her son at Giza rather than with her husband at Dahshur? Second, if this was indeed the burial place of Hetepheres, then why, when the sarcophagus was opened, was it found to be empty?

The excavator of the tomb, George Reisner, suggested answers to both these questions. He thought that Hetepheres and her furniture had originally been buried in a satellite pyramid next to the Red Pyramid at Dahshur. However, soon after she was buried her tomb was broken into and ransacked by thieves who stole her body. When news of this reached the vizier (the governor of this area), he panicked. As the person in charge of security, he would be in serious trouble if the new king, Khufu, heard that the body of his mother had been stolen. Consequently, the vizier ordered the lid put back on the empty sarcophagus, and he pretended that Hetepheres' body was still inside the box! Everybody then agreed that it would be safer for her coffin to be transferred to Giza and rehidden in a new tomb.

We know that this really was Hetepheres' burial site because of discoveries made in an alabaster box or chest hidden on a small shelf in the room. The inside of this chest was divided into four compartments. One of these contained dry organic matter in the bottom, and the other three had a yellowish liquid. This liquid was analyzed and proved to be natron, a material used for embalming, and also the remains of the internal organs of the queen.

These finds are the best evidence that we have for furniture and funerary equipment during the Old Kingdom. They are all beautifully made and decorated, and all show a high degree of skill in carpentry and gold working. The canopy is one of the things illustrated in paintings from the predynastic period onward. It was designed to be hung with mats or with curtains, both to ensure privacy and to keep mosquitoes away while sleeping. A box for storing the curtains was found next to the poles of the canopy. The bed had an inlaid footboard and a silver covered headrest. Egyptian beds sloped down toward the foot end. Two chairs were found, but only one could be completely reconstructed. This has a wide, low seat and decorated side and back panels. There is another chair on poles for carrying the queen, and there are also various boxes covered with elaborate decorations. One of these contained twenty silver bracelets arranged in two rows. These are all decorated with butterflies made of blue lapis lazuli, red carnelian, and green turquoise. The label on the box reads "box containing rings" and "Mother of the King of Upper and Lower Egypt Hetepheres," and a painting of Hetepheres from the back of the other incomplete chair shows her wearing rows of bracelets just like the ones found.

THE BOATING PARTY

That Snefru was remembered as a kind and happy king by later generations is illustrated in a story that was told nearly a thousand years later. This was written down on a document now called the Westcar Papyrus.

A painted relief sculpture of a flute player accompanying a singer during a performance for the pharaoh.

One day King Snefru was bored and wandered through all the rooms of the palace in search of something to do. He summoned one of the men who worked in his household, saying, "Go, bring me the chief lector priest, the scribe of books, Djadja-em-ankh." The tale says, "He was brought to him straight away. His majesty said to him 'I have gone through all the rooms of the palace in search of relaxation and found none.' Djadja-em-ankh said to him 'May your majesty proceed to the lake of the palace. Fill a boat with all the beautiful girls of your palace. Your majesty's heart will be refreshed by seeing them row up and down. As

A painted plaster panel showing geese feeding on grass

you observe the fine nesting places of your lake, as you observe its beautiful fields and shores, your heart will be refreshed.'"

The king was very pleased by this idea, and replied, "Let there be brought to me twenty women with the shapeliest bodies, breasts and braids, who have not yet given birth. Also let there be brought to me twenty nets and give these nets to the women in place of their clothes." The girls did as they were told, and "they rowed up and down, and his majesty's heart was happy seeing them row." However, one of the girls dropped her new turquoise necklace over the side of the boat, and when

Snefru said, "Row! I shall replace it for you," the girl replied, "I prefer my thing to one like it." So the king summoned Djadja-em-ankh once more, and the priest cast a spell that "placed one side of the lake's water upon the other," and he then found the pendant lying on a stone on the bottom of the lake. The story ends with: "His majesty spent the day feasting with the entire palace. Then he rewarded the chief lector priest Djadja-em-ankh with all good things."

GLOSSARY

cataract A region of rapids and turbulent waters on a fast-flowing river.

cubit The main unit of distance measurement in ancient Egypt. Approximately the length of a man's forearm. The cubit was divided into seven palm widths.

cultivation The season between September and April during which crops were planted and ripened.

dynasty A succession of rulers from the same family or line. Egyptian history was divided into thirty-one dynasties stretching from King Menes in the First Dynasty up to the invasion of Alexander the Great in 332 BC.

harvest The season between April and June when crops were harvested.

inundation The season of the annual flooding of the Nile, which took place between June and September.

ka The soul, or life force, of every ancient Egyptian. A person's *ka* was born at the same time as the person and existed throughout his or her life. When an individual died, the *ka* continued to live on. This then needed feeding and looking after, which led to the development of funerary cults, where either food and drink, or pictures of food and drink, were offered to the *ka*.

kemet The name for Egypt that the ancient Egyptians used. The word means "black land." This refers to fertile Nile mud that was washed across the land every year when the river flooded in a season called the inundation.

king list A group of carvings or paintings listing the names and titles of former kings in succession. Most lists have been found in tombs or temples, and they were usually written to justify a present ruler's claim to the throne by showing him making offerings to his ancestors.

Lower Egypt The northern half of the country stretching from Memphis, near modern-day Cairo, to the Mediterranean coast.

Maat A goddess who embodied aspects of truth, justice, and harmony in the universe. The power of Maat regulated the seasons and the movement of the sun, the moon, and the stars. One of the main jobs of the king was to maintain the rule of Maat.

FOR MORE INFORMATION

ORGANIZATIONS

American Research Center in Egypt
  (U.S. Office)
Emory University West Campus
1256 Briarcliff Road, NE
Building A, Suite 423W
Atlanta, GA 30322
(404) 712-9854
e-mail: arce@emory.edu

International Association of
  Egyptologists (USA Branch)
Department of Ancient Egyptian,
  Nubian, and Far Eastern Art
Museum of Fine Arts
465 Huntington Avenue
Boston, MA 02115

JOURNALS

Ancient Egypt magazine
Empire House
1 Newton Street
Manchester M1 1HW
England
e-mail: empire@globalnet.co.uk

WEB SITES
Due to the changing nature of Internet links, the Rosen Publishing Group, Inc., has developed an online list of Web sites related to the subject of this book. This site is updated regularly. Please use this link to access the list:

http://www.rosenlinks.com/lae/snef/

For FURTHER READING

Aldred, Cyril. *The Egyptians*. London & New York: Thames & Hudson, 1998.

Arnold, Dorothea. *When the Pyramids Were Built: Egyptian Art in the Old Kingdom*. New York: Metropolitan Museum of Art, 1999.

Baines, John, and Jaromir Malek. *Atlas of Ancient Egypt*. New York: Facts on File, 1993.

Davies, Vivian, and Renee Friedman. *Egypt Uncovered*. New York: Stewart, Tabori & Chang, 1998.

Edwards, I.E.S. *The Pyramids of Egypt*. New York: Penguin, 1985.

Malek, Jaromir. *In the Shadow of the Pyramids: Egypt During the Old Kingdom*. Norman, OK: University of Oklahoma Press, 1992.

Shaw, Ian. *Egyptian Warfare and Weapons*. Princes Risborough, England: Shire, 1991.

Shaw, Ian, and Paul Nicholson. *British Museum Dictionary of Ancient Egypt.* London: British Museum Press, 1995.

Watson, Philip. *Egyptian Pyramids and Mastaba Tombs.* Princes Risborough, England: Shire, 1987.

BIBLIOGRAPHY

Breasted, James. *Ancient Records of Egypt Vol. I: The First through Seventeenth Dynasties.* Chicago: University of Chicago Press, 2001

Egyptian Art in the Age of the Pyramids. New York: Exhibition Catalogue, Metropolitan Museum of Art, 1999

Fakhry, Ahmed. *The Monuments of Sneferu at Dahshur.* (2 vols.). Cairo: General Organisation for Government Printing Offices, 1959 & 1961.

Hayes, William. *The Scepter of Egypt I: From the Earliest Times to the End of the Middle Kingdom.* New York: Metropolitan Museum of Art, 1990

Lehner, Mark. *The Complete Pyramids.* London & New York: Thames & Hudson, 1997.

Lichtheim, Miriam. *Ancient Egyptian Literature Volume I: The Old and Middle Kingdoms.* Berkeley: UCLA Press, 1975.

Reisner, George, and William Stevenson Smith. *A History of the Giza Necropolis Volume II.* Cambridge, MA: Harvard Press, 1955.

INDEX

ABOUT THE AUTHOR

Susanna Thomas has a B.A. in Egyptian archaeology from University College, London, and was awarded a Ph.D. from Liverpool University in 2000. She has worked sites all over Egypt, including in the Valley of the Kings, and runs excavations at Tell Abqa'in in the western Delta. She is particularly interested in vitreous materials and trade in the late Bronze Age. She is currently a research fellow at Liverpool University and director of the Ramesside Fortress Town Project.

CREDITS